96 1396

CHRISTIAN LACROIX

Translated from the French by Saron Hughes

First Published in Great Britain in 1996
by Thames and Hudson Ltd, London

British Library Cataloguing-in-Publication Data

A catalogue record for this book is available from the British Library

ISBN 0-500-01764-6

Printed and bound in Italy

CHRISTIAN LACROIX

TEXT BY FRANÇOIS BAUDOT

THAMES AND HUDSON

h

aute couture was born of the flamboyant opulence of the nineteenth century. It has not always been around, and it may not be around for much longer. So Christian Lacroix finds himself in the curious position of being the last in a long line of great couturiers, poised between two rapidly diverging worlds and modes of production.

From its beginnings during the Second Empire through to the Second World War, haute couture developed into a thriving labour industry. It achieved giddy heights with the launch of the New Look in 1947 and was eventually raised to the status of high art, while at the same time manufacturing processes were being increasingly perfected. By the beginning of the 1980s, haute couture seemed to be entering into the final stages of its evolution.

At that time, and subsequently, the prevailing feeling seemed to be that fashions for young people should be created by young designers dedicated to the biannual renewal of ready-to-wear consumer trends. So when Lacroix came on the scene in the mid-eighties he performed a dramatic *coup de théâtre*, chiefly by being open and positive about his allegiance to haute couture. It was a conviction which led him to open a couture house in his own name and to found it on the strict observance of antiquated rules which had been established by a profession given up for dead.

S trange as it may seem, Lacroix was not only successful in finding a financial backer, Bernard Arnault, who gave shape to this dream, but his house also became an instant hit with the public. What had been achieved by another designer, also called Christian, after the Liberation, was being accomplished all over again. Then, it had been Christian Dior, whose couture house is today owned by the same group which backs Lacroix. It would appear that the fashion industry must periodically undergo violent, completely unpredictable upheavals, even though this unpredictability is itself one of the founding principles of the business.

In any case, Lacroix, the youngest descendant of haute couture, awoke the Sleeping Beauty of fashion and radically altered the accepted rules governing its development at the end of the twentieth century. He did this by embracing nostalgia, by employing an idiosyncratic approach which contravened the rules of marketing, and by acting on the whim of the moment. Whether we like it or not, there is and always will be in the long history of style a period 'before Lacroix' and a period 'after Lacroix'. This has little to do with the quality of his sources of inspiration or what they produce. Its truth resides in his attitude, which is both exuberant and melancholic, caustic and tender, timeless and brilliant. It is a truth born of our times, times in which paradox has sounded the death blow to certainty, where appearances have replaced philosophy, and where unexpected encounters – the

umbrella and sewing machine on the operating table, for example –
have become the stuff of everyday life. Only in such daft times could a
perfume be called: *C'est la Vie!*

Christian Lacroix has always insisted, right from the start, that
he was never concerned with 'fashion'; the only fashion he
followed was his own. At odds with contemporary trends, his
ideal woman is one who is accountable only to her mirror. She mixes
together different styles as she travels through different countries:
places which the designer is careful not to visit himself before incorpo-
rating their exoticism into his collections. This independent look is
created from woven, interwoven and collaged elements. In this way,
revolution is replaced by juxtaposition – of looks, of styles and of refer-
ences. Rather than making a tabula rasa of the past, Christian Lacroix
takes it on and pushes it about in order to anticipate what tomorrow
might bring. More than the clothes of any other designer, Lacroix's
carry with them a sense of regret for the feeling that inspired them. In
contrast to much of contemporary fashion, which has been designed
especially for the camera and then reproduced by it, no photograph
could accurately re-create the experience of watching one of Lacroix's
dresses go by. For him, couture is a dream which cannot be contained.
It cannot be canned or reheated, and reproductions do not do it justice.
And yet perhaps it is because of this very irreducibility, which is so
often lacking from our *fin-de-siècle* standardization, that the value of
such an attitude as Lacroix's is now being appreciated. Since he is one
of the last remaining upholders of free-spirited fashion, it is to Lacroix's
way of thinking that we must now look if we are to regain a stylishness
and individuality which has been sacrificed rather too hastily for the
benefit of the many.

because of its continual self-renewal, fashion is about the transitory, just as, throughout his collections, Christian Lacroix uses a vocabulary that continually constructs and deconstructs itself. How better to illustrate it than by an alphabetical guide? His hieroglyphics borrow from sources as diverse as Byzantium and Cecil Beaton; he goes from the salt marshes of the Camargue to the seediest parts of London; from flea markets to the markets in Provence; from Jacques-Henri Lartigue's paintings and photographs to scenes from *Banana Split*. His sources include the circus, the music hall and the amphitheatre; films by Max Ophuls or Jacques Demy; Las Meninas and the Moors of El Escorial; the last Kings of Africa; the former Princess of Wales; the sixties . . . Lacroix himself says: 'I think we often only have one thing to say . . . but this one thing is continually evolving. It is this constancy within change which determines a style . . . Couture will always be couture . . . crazy, contradictory, full of surprises and – above all – stronger than I am.'

An A to Z guide to Christian Lacroix

A

ARLES: This sleepy town in the Bouches-du-Rhône region, nestled on the northern tip of the Camargue between its marshes, grasslands and the Alpilles mountains, is where Christian Lacroix spent his solitary infancy, cradled in its ancient walls. He was born in May 1951 under the particularly symbolic sign of Taurus. The enduring traditions of this former Roman colony, with its magnificent remains, lively amphitheatre, proud language and strong sense of identity, provided the designer with a heritage which he would continually draw upon. Never before had Parisian fashion flaunted its origins in quite this way, attracting the eyes of the world to this little enclave of sunshine, holidays and cicadas. Provence is known as the place of the ultimate return. Since Alphonse

Daudet first wrote about Provençal life, it has regularly attracted the likes of Jean Cocteau, some Royal Highness or other craving the simple life, and the wealthy pensioner weary of the Cote d'Azur and its mirages, all of whom come to its poor, sunbaked lands which have been cultivated by three thousand years of civilization.

B

BEATON: If Lacroix's main sources of inspiration had to be identified, one of them would be the photographs, or rather the entire diaphanous oeuvre, of Sir Cecil Beaton. A costume and set designer, make-up artist and photographer, Beaton created visual arguments throughout the twentieth century for his judgments on style, elegance and the art of living. A true dandy, he struck a fine balance between the aristocratic and the conservative on the one hand, and the coolly relaxed, extravagant and cosmopolitan on the other.

C

THE CAMARGUE: A mirage of sky, lagoons and grasslands, the Camargue countryside, unlike the more distinctive Provence, provided an ideal metaphysical backdrop for the designer, allowing him to project onto it whatever he wished. As a result he always seems to be somewhere else: in cowboy country as seen by Picasso, steeped in gypsy witchcraft and with strange ruins strewn on its white sands.

D

DIOR: In the world of haute couture, Christian Lacroix has most in common with Christian Dior. Although from immeasurably different times, they both share the same unexpected thrust into the limelight, the same small-town shyness and good manners, the same determination mixed with uncertainty, and the same respect for tradition and good craftsmanship. With their nonconformist talents, both defy definition, their notoriety seemingly in inverse proportion to their contempt for media attention.

E

ESPAÑA: This secluded country, characterized by excess and anachronism, is one of Christian Lacroix's passions. From its grandeur to its simplicity; its bullfights to its great paintings; from Carmen's skirts, the matador's cape, or the barefoot Ava Gardner to Hemingway's novels, Lacroix seeks out its legends and traditions and borrows from them. His sources can include anything from the black Spanish dress with its air of princely poverty, lace mantillas, blood- and sweat-stained jaquetillas with their clashing harmonies of black and white and their golden embroidery, to a coat by Balenciaga or a blouse by Madame Irma.

F

FRANÇOISE: As a happily married man, Lacroix yet again stands out from the fashion crowd. He shares his life with Françoise, whom he met by chance twenty years ago. At that time he was still a young provincial, studying at the Ecole du Louvre in order to become a museum conservator. Together, he and Françoise lived through the fashion euphoria which took hold of the late seventies, and finally decided that they too would join in the adventure. Their fruitful dialogue soon brought results. He is by nature taciturn and a worrier, while she is always alert and finds nothing too much of a challenge. This was all it took for them to get married and create, late at night in bed and in fits of giggles, a world all of their own.

G

GYPSY KINGS: Under the old bridge which links Arles with Trinquetaille, the quiet suburb where Lacroix was born, there is a permanent encampment of caravans surrounded by lines of washing. This is where the group The Gypsy Kings was formed. These young gypsies, who started off busking for loose change in cafes, went on to conquer the Top 50 and the United States, and finally to make their fortune. Their success came in the same summer that the Lacroix couture house opened, in July 1987, with the triumphal fashion show which was hailed as marking the rebirth of haute couture. To end it, The Gypsy Kings, who had come up specially from the Midi, made the whole of Paris dance all night long, and in the months which followed. People said the music was just another passing fashion, but for the first time in a long while it was music which owed nothing either to French traditions or to rhythms from across the Atlantic. It was like a return to a Europe without frontiers; something neither Christian Lacroix nor these temporarily wealthy gypsies were strangers to.

H

HAUTE COUTURE: 'What purpose does it serve?' is a question often asked of Christian Lacroix, who invariably replies: 'None.' After all, there is more to life than things which serve a purpose! But it is true that the general enthusiasm which surrounded the setting up of Lacroix's couture house does indicate in retrospect that it came at the right time – which is the number one rule in fashion. And yet how is it that everyone can simultaneously and independently agree in their praise of something that they would have run a mile from only six months earlier? Well, that's Paris for you, and it is the reason why so many designers always go there to put their ideas to the test.

I

INTRA MUROS: Like many towns in the Midi, Arles is in the form of a citadel, within whose enclosing walls the dreams of its inhabitants have developed. An intense internal life and a certain decorum prevail. There is a natural affinity between people's houses and what they wear, and Christian Lacroix himself has always been as interested in architecture as in fashion. While flicking through faded fashion journals in the loft at home, he came across a batch of old *Plaisir de France* magazines. At the age of fifteen he was bowled over by the character Des Esseintes, hero of the novel *A Rebours* by J.K. Huysmans, and today has proved himself to be a true decorative arts historian. This is evident from the brilliant book he produced with Patrick Mauriès which combines both drawing and text in a carefully compiled list of different decorative styles expressive of our time (published by Le Promeneur in *Styles d'aujourd'hui*). For the fitting-out of his couture house ten years ago, Lacroix entrusted the job to two relative newcomers who afterwards became known as the epitome of the new French artist–designers: Elisabeth Garouste and Mattia Bonetti.

J

JEAN-JACQUES: Inseparably bound up with the Christian Lacroix story is Jean-Jacques Picart, a publicity officer first and foremost and an advisor on all manner of French luxury goods. In 1978 he had Lacroix brought in to Hermès, where he acquired the skills necessary to become an assistant to the designer Guy Paulin. It was again through Picart that Lacroix took up the haute-couture cause, this time at Patou. In 1986 their work was officially recognized when they won their first Dé d'Or, and in the following year in New York, the CFDA (Council of Fashion Designers of America) award for the most influential foreign designer. Finally, with the help of Bernard Arnault, they went into partnership and founded the House of Lacroix in a beautiful eighteenth-century *hôtel particulier* at 73 Rue du Faubourg Saint-Honoré. Much more than a faithful second-in-command, Picart was a paradigm of self-sufficiency and competence, handling the management of studios and workshops, as well as promotion and everything else that goes into the smooth running of a couture house.

K

KITSCH: In order to save haute couture from the stranglehold of good taste, its rules had to be broken and its assumptions questioned. By the eighties, an 'innate sense of the beautiful' was paralyzing rather than stimulating French design. Lacroix was a child of May '68, brought up on irony, mix-and-match utopianism and second-hand goods, and kitsch was part of his inheritance, while his sense of being at one remove allowed him to maintain a certain detachment. It enabled him to conjure up an entire universe out of everything and out of nothing, mixing different styles and periods with complete disregard for rules – rules which, in any case, kitsch had long since blown to pieces.

L

LONDON: Whether from direct experience or not, London symbolizes for the French a state of mind which has much to do with kitsch (see above). Every French person has his or her own perception of England, gleaned first and foremost from the ubiquitous pop song with its rudimentary language lessons. It is typified by tweed, the twist, riots, the Swinging Sixties, vampires in crushed velvet, bowler hats and leather boots. Fashion has never actively been discouraged here; it has simply never existed. In its place there has been an acceptance of the most mutually antagonistic styles, from the Queen Mother to the Sex Pistols. Christian Lacroix first visited London when he was sixteen or seventeen years old. He has returned again and again to the city, whose spectacular diversity has encouraged him to conquer his own limitations.

M

MODE: In describing the women of Arles during the sixties (quoted in a collection of memoirs published by Thames and Hudson called *Pieces of a Pattern*), Lacroix says:

'Only one of these women, distant and mysterious, seemed to take pleasure in flouting this grey/white/black/beige tradition. There can be no doubt that it was the influence of her scarlet suits, her stiletto heels, her panther toques and collars, her make-up in shades of bronze, her enormous earrings and her crisp, short hairstyles that made me understand what fashion really was: an elegance that makes itself noticed.'

N

NOSTALGIA: Time and again Christian Lacroix finds his inspiration for his clothes, accessories and traditional, ageless jewelry in the past and in other lands. Without a second thought, he combines sophistication with elements from disappearing cultures, imaginary rituals and raw and naive primitive art. His love of the extravagant attracts him to the extremes that fashion can reach in times of crisis: the ultramodish Incroyables and the Merveilleuses of the Directoire period; or the costumes from the Ballets Russes which made their mark on the eve of the First World War; or the Occupation style during World War II. Throughout the twentieth century right up until the 1980s, the past, symbolizing conservatism, has been considered in opposition to the future, which symbolizes hope. The Lacroix phenomenon has certainly contributed – at least in France – to the revising of this over-simplistic duality. Nostalgia has therefore become one of the generative forces of the decade, in which the word 'restoration' has been replaced by 'rehabilitation'.

O

OPERA: Although Lacroix rarely moved around when he was young, he was at heart a travelling performer. He lived in Saintes-Maries-de-la-Mer alongside gypsy caravans and was filled with wonder at the small fairground theatres. Ever since, he has had a passion for the world of music and theatre. This is a continuing thread in his work and it surfaces in his shows, which are received like virtuoso arias. Lacroix is haunted by what Cocteau described as: 'le mal rouge et or du theatre' ('the red and gold malaise of the theatre'), basking in the occasional splendours of the festivals at Aix, Orange and Avignon. 'Theatre for me was above all what I did for myself. As a child I enjoyed making costumes and putting them on little cardboard cut-out figures. I would then redesign the costumes when I came back from the theatre.' It was only much later, when he showed these drawings to Françoise, whom he had just met, that he found out from her how close they were to the designs then being presented in shows by the so-called 'young designers' of 1978. And so from theatre to fashion was but one step. Persuaded by his wife, Lacroix hastily put together a folio which he showed to a few well-known designers. Their encouragement, his meeting with Jean-Jacques Picart and about ten years of training did the rest.

P

PATCHWORK: If Lacroix's contribution to the development of fashion had to be summed up in one word, it would be patchwork. His needlework ranges from the modest to the sumptuous, assembling pieces of material, like complex fragments of a collective memory, into a primitive or sophisticated design. A luxury for the poor and a pastime for the lonely, patchwork can also be found today in some of the major museums. But from collage to juxtaposition, and from scratching to remixes by today's disc-jockeys, the principle of the unexpected connection is still one which enriches and underpins our times.

Q

QUALITY: As practised by designers such as Christian Lacroix, haute couture today signifies less a corporate body or category than a certain quality. The difference, like that between a thoroughbred and a horse with no pedigree, is perceptible only to the initiated.

R

REMINISCENCE: Lacroix is at heart a romantic. Pushed from the nest, driven from his quiet home town, torn from his books and papers and his precious studies by that insatiable animal, fashion, the designer sought protection by immersing himself in the not-too-distant past. Since living in the here-and-now can be the quickest way to age fashion, Lacroix wisely prefers to achieve a greater timelessness by reliving a semi-imaginary past.

S

SPECTACLE: See Opera.

T

TIME: In February 1988, at the time of the launch of his second haute-couture collection, Christian Lacroix appeared on the cover of *Time* magazine. In the United States this is considered a distinction equal to France's Légion d'Honneur. The only other fashion designers to enjoy such publicity before the young Lacroix were the legendary Christian Dior and Giorgio Armani, king of Italian ready-to-wear. Miraculously, all have survived the exposure.

U

UNIVERSE: Almost ten years on from its beginnings, an entire universe has formed around the Lacroix couture house through successive aggregates. In March 1988, Lacroix showed his first ready-to-wear line, followed the year after by accessories. Then, in 1990, the perfume *C'est la Vie!* was launched. More shops were opened in addition to the one on the ground floor of his couture house: in Avenue Montaigne (1991), in Place Saint Sulpice (1995) and in Aix, Salzburg, Avignon, Toulouse, London, New York, Japan and, of course, Arles-sur-Rhône. The sportswear collection, Bazar, was launched in 1994 followed by furnishing fabrics in 1995 and jeans the year after. Meanwhile, the couturier was preparing a new perfume and continuing to design costumes for the stage, his most recent collaborations being *Othello* at Théâtre 14 and *Phèdre* at the Comédie Française in 1995.

V

THE VIRGIN: Reliquaries in southern Italy, 'santi belli' (painted terracotta statuettes made in Provence in the nineteenth century for domestic altars), the pilgrimage town of Saintes-Maries-de-la-Mer, the Macarena of Seville in all her layers of veils and piles of precious jewels: Lacroix sees all these Marian icons, from the good mother to the Black Virgin, as his guardian angels. His wedding dresses in particular are inspired by the figure of the Virgin, but more generally she represents his sense of the sacred and his superstitiousness – like that of the matador who crosses himself before lunging at the bull.

W

WINDSOR: In diametrical opposition to this dazzling Virgin is the venomous figure of the Duchess of Windsor, who symbolizes for Lacroix the dark, more seductive side of womankind. Relentlessly sophisticated, for her the realities of life always give way to the demands of dream. Generally, designers today like to dress actresses, showbusiness stars and top models. Christian Lacroix's dresses are undoubtedly the last which are destined for what is essentially an endangered species: queens. Even those without crowns.

X.Y.Z

X Y ZAPPING: The word, though ugly, has at least the advantage of being easily understood. Channel surfing, or *le zapping* as it is called in France, is an activity from which few of us escape. However, you need to know how to use this patchwork of sounds and images, how to pick out new ideas from what is in fact a jumble, and all the more ephemeral for being so. Christian Lacroix's style, particularly in the variety of his haute-couture collections, offers a fashion equivalent to this cultivated zapping which, whether for pleasure or by necessity, all of us practise today who travel on, learn from, watch and capture these waves of chaos – like a fly's multifaceted eye, trained on a world where everything changes, except change itself.

49

48

50

51

MONA

A. BAYLE

KARINA

KAZUSHA N!

52

53

54

55

56

ACEVE

MAN

D. di MI

A. BAYLE

38

39

60

41

42

KARINA

T. B

ACEVE

T. B.

MONNA

43

44

45

46

47

FLORENCE

KARINA

LAWRENCE

A. ROART

SUZANNA

pour Antonio Banderas Chroma à la

gold
embro

cuir brodé sur f...
sur fond foncé

Christian Lacroix

P/AP.

col très étroit et bas

épaules tombantes raglan

petite croisure 6 petits boutons

décolleté très profond

droite puis évasée aux petites hanches

mon-cher 314

96

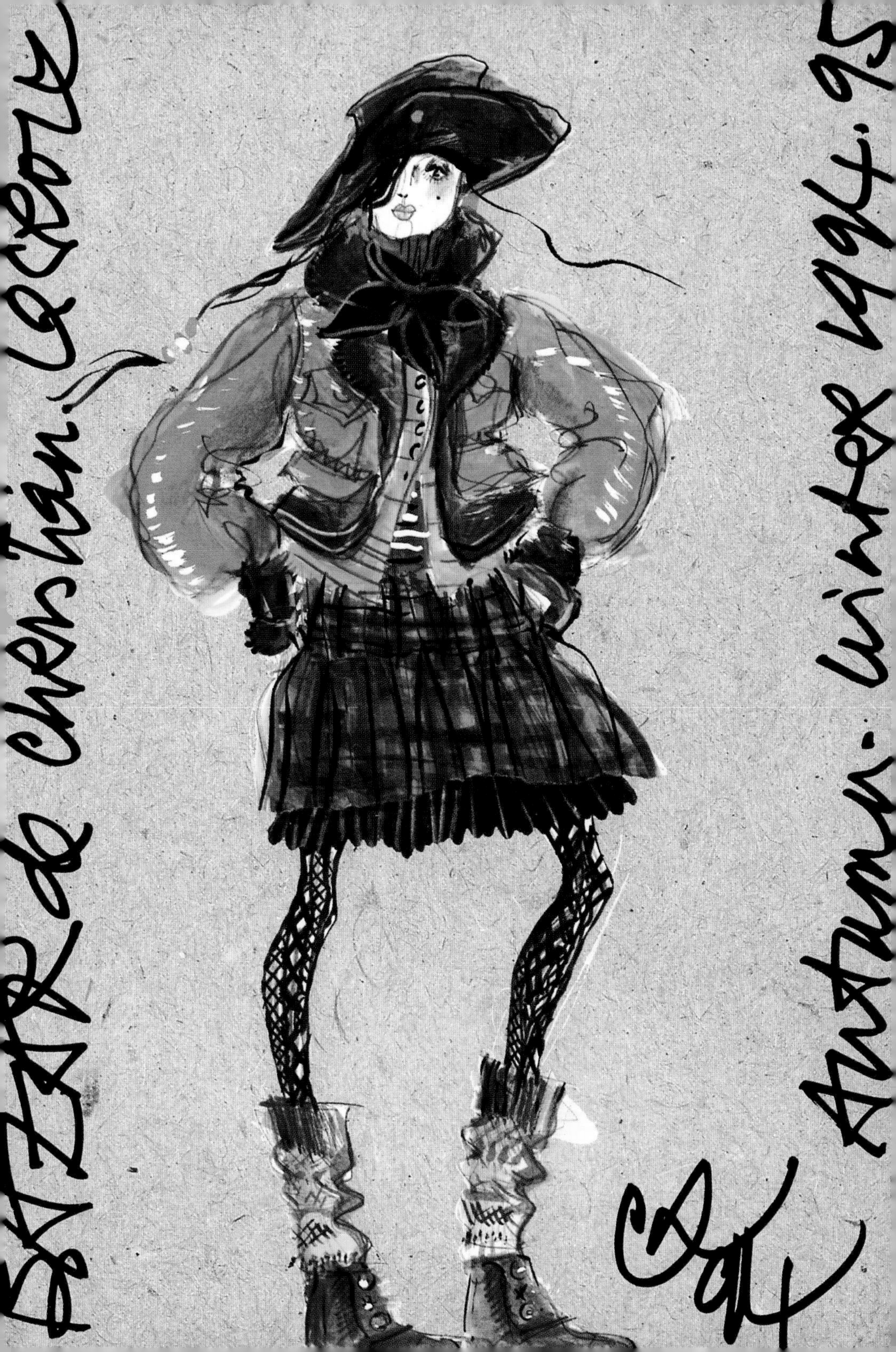
Bazar de Christian Lacroix
Autumn-Winter 95

FEBRUARY 8, 1988

TIME

No. 6

ISRAEL
Crisis of
Conscience

Fantasy
Comes
Alive!

Voilà...
French
Designer
Christian
Lacroix

AUSTRIA	S 30	GERMANY	DM 4.50	ISRAEL (incl. tax)	NS 3.50	NORWAY	Kr 16.00	SWITZERLAND	F 4.00
BELGIUM	F 100	GIBRALTAR	£1.25	ITALY	Lit 3200	PORTUGAL	Esc 270	UNITED KINGDOM	£1.20
DENMARK	Kr 17.00	GREECE	Dr 280	LUXEMBOURG	F 100	SPAIN	Pta 300	U.S. ARMED FORCES	$2.25
FINLAND	Mk 12.00	ICELAND (incl. tax)	Kr 75.00	NETHERLANDS	Fl 5.00	SWEDEN	Kr 16.00	YUGOSLAVIA	ND 2000
FRANCE	F 16.00	IRELAND (incl. tax)	IR£1.30						WEEKLY

flower girl

G 01/87

Chronology

1951   Born on 16 May in Arles (Bouches-du-Rhône).

1973   Having discovered a passion for drawing at an early age, Lacroix goes to the Sorbonne, Paris, and to the Ecole du Louvre, where he writes a dissertation on seventeenth-century costume and takes an examination in museum conservation.

1978   Starts work at Hermès, where he learns the basic skills. Here he becomes assistant to Guy Paulin.

1980   Collaborates with the couturier of the Imperial Court, Tokyo.

1981   Christian Lacroix, with Jean-Jacques Picart, starts work for Jean Patou as head of Haute Couture.

1986   Lacroix is awarded his first Dé d'Or.

1987   In January, the CFDA (Council of Fashion Designers of America) give him the award for the most influential foreign designer.
Meets Bernard Arnault and they go into partnership to found the House of Christian Lacroix at 73 Rue du Faubourg Saint-Honoré.
Fashion show in July of the first collection of Haute Couture, dedicated to the Midi.
Designs by Lacroix for *Tarnished Angels* by Karol Armitage at the Opéra, Paris (Garnier).

1988   He is awarded his second Dé d'Or, in January, for his second collection.
Launch in March of his first ready-to-wear line.
Designs the costumes for *Gaieté Parisienne* by Mikhail Baryshnikov at the Metropolitan Opera in New York.

1989   Launch of his line of Accessories.
Designs the costumes for *Carmen* at the amphitheatre in Nîmes.

1990   Launch of perfume *C'est la Vie!*

1991   Opening of new boutique in Avenue Montaigne, Paris.

1992   Designs the costumes for *L'As-tu Revue?* by Jacques Offenbach at the Opéra Comique in Paris.
Publication of his book, *Pieces of a Pattern*.

1994   Designs a new collection plus some sportswear under the name 'Bazar'.

1995   Launch of fabrics and a line called *Jeans*.
Designs the costumes for *Othello* at the Théâtre 14, and for *Phèdre* at the Comédie Française, in Paris.

1996   Publication of *Christian Lacroix: The Diary of a Collection*, by Patrick Mauriès, reproducing scrapbooks kept by Christian Lacroix in the run-up to his Spring/Summer 1994 collection.

Backstage at a ready-to-wear fashion show: Nadège, Christian Lacroix and Jean-Jacques Picart, who glances back at the audience for one last time. Photo © Abbas/Magnum.

Christian Lacroix

Influence of the South. Lacroix finds the inspiration for his jewelry and accessories mainly in provincial France and in traditional costumes from all over the world. Brooch 1989. Photo © Laziz Hamani.

A tribute. The entire audience applauded this wedding dress when it appeared at the 1987 show. It was the first Lacroix and his fashion house had designed, with a short black velvet jacket embroidered by Lesage with an ex-voto, over a 'meringue' skirt in ivory damask silk. Photo © Javier Vallhonrat.

The first triumphant success of the Lacroix style: the transposition of Provençal culture into haute couture. Cropped velvet jacket with the Camargue cross embroidered in golden thread on the back. The cross symbolizes faith; the heart, love; and the anchor, hope. The skirt is based on a caparison, the quilted covering used to protect the flanks of a picador's horse during a bullfight. Autumn/Winter Haute Couture Collection 1987–88. Photo © all rights reserved. On the right: a sketch for the same dress, christened 'Feria' and presented in July 1987. © Christian Lacroix.

Mixed influences: a cross between 18th-century Arles and the fifties. This Haute Couture dress, from the 1987–88 season, was christened 'Cigale' (cicada) and is made from black lace with a striped satin skirt, lace facing and a red satin fichu. Photo © Jean-François Gaté.

From long to short. The first Haute Couture Collection, July 1987: the initial designs were for a long dress, but the final version was short. Drawing © Christian Lacroix.

The mini crinoline. Strapless dress with shawl worn round the shoulders 'à l'arlesiénne', with a defined waist and open skirt which allows the legs to move freely. This is Lacroix's version of the eighties Parisian woman. The dress is in duchesse satin with pinafore in chartreuse duchesse satin. Part of the publicity campaign for the first Haute Couture Collection, July 1987. Photo © Javier Vallhonrat.

'Magnanarelle' (Provençal dialect for a breeder of silkworms). Pinafore dress in black faille dotted with violets, for Christian Lacroix's first Haute Couture Collection, July 1987. Photo © Javier Vallhonrat.

In the wings of the project: storyboard of Christian Lacroix's first Haute Couture Collection, Winter 1987–88 (July 1987).

Long skirt in white faille appliquéd with velvet motifs, worn with a simple sweater and heavy jewels in gilt metal with red trimming. Ready-to-Wear catalogue, Autumn/Winter 1992–93. © Photo Tyen.

For the most recently born couture house, a completely new décor was needed. This photograph shows Christian Lacroix, his wife Françoise (on the sofa) and Jean-Jacques Picart (standing behind) in the rooms decorated by Elizabeth Garouste and Mattia Bonetti according to Christian Lacroix's instructions. Photo Gilles de Chabaneix. © SCOOP/*Elle*.

'Postscript'. Detail of a long dress with bustier in black lace and chiffon, gathered to look like a jacket. Haute Couture 1991–92. Photo © Dominique Issermann.

Ink-coloured dress. An evening gown in metallic silk with bodice embroidered in stones. Photo © Marc Hispard – SCOOP/*Elle* No. 2614.

Kadija, the African beauty, wears the 'Maja' design: with loose corolla top in chocolate faille and satin velvet skirt with 'Pompeii' print. Haute Couture Autumn/Winter 1988–89.
Lacroix's muse and model, Marie Seznec, today the director of his Haute Couture salons, wears the 'Diabolo' dress in black velvet with black faille sleeves. Autumn/Winter 1988–89. For both: Photo © Tiziano Magni/*Air France Madame* No. 7, 1988.

Irving Penn, one of the world's greatest fashion photographers, has captured in this one image all the mastery Lacroix has achieved after ten years of relentless and prolific work. Evening dress with leg-of-mutton sleeve in vanilla duchesse satin, inspired by Boldine. Photo © Irving Penn. Courtesy of *Vogue*. Copyright © 1995 by the Condé Nast Publications, Inc.

A tribute to the 'Merveilleuses' of the late eighteenth century. Shalom Harlow poses here in an Empire-line coat in tulle and écru lace worn over an ivory satin bodice.
Sent to the four corners of the globe: Christian Lacroix's wedding dresses, which have become his speciality, are packaged in a manner befitting their elegance. Here is a shimmering tulle confection, with a detachable pleated taffeta train. Both photographs are by Irving Penn. Courtesy of *Vogue*. Copyright © 1995 by the Condé Nast Publications, Inc.

Wedding dress with satin bodice embroidered with a heart, over tulle dress with detachable train. Photo © Steven Meisel/A+C Anthology. This photograph was originally published in American *Vogue*.

The fresh country air of the eighteenth century combined with a masterful savoir-faire: the essence of Christian Lacroix is distilled in this wedding veil embroidered by Lesage, which closed his eighteenth Haute Couture Collection in January 1996. Photo © Paolo Roversi.
Ancestral links. Photographed around 1920, the couturier's great-aunts pose in the costumes the women of Arles used to wear. © Thames and Hudson Ltd. /Collection Christian Lacroix.

A source of inspiration. This was one of the paintings the young Lacroix used to admire at the Musée Réattu in Arles, long before he decided to become a fashion designer, and its influence can be found in his first personal collections. It is a late-18th-century painting by Antoine Raspal, entitled *Atelier de Couture* (oil on wood. 32.5 x 40.5 cm). © Musée Réattu, Arles. Photo B. Delgado.

Beauty on a rail. Outfits from the Haute Couture Spring/Summer Collection 1991. Photo © Noëlle Hoeppe. *Air France Madame* No. 22, April/May 1991.
Lobster red. Christy Turlington wears a shimmering taffeta caraco with a puff collar and sleeves over a bell-shaped calf-length skirt. Haute Couture Autumn/Winter 1991–92. Photo © Roxanne Lowit.

High-heeled lace-up shoes, 'Balayeuse' (or 'roadsweeper' petticoat) in black tulle, under a calf-length Chinese lantern skirt in draped salmon taffeta, with brown velvet bodice and red duchesse satin sleeves, from the Autumn/Winter Haute Couture Collection 1987–88. Photos © all rights reserved/*Air France Madame* No.4, 1987.

Toreador. Sketches by Christian Lacroix from 1991 for a bullfighter's costume worn by Chamaco for his investiture as a matador in the amphitheatre in Nîmes, 1992; the meeting of haute-couture dreams with the blood and sweat of the amphitheatre. © Christian Lacroix.

The famous toreador Chamaco in his ceremonial costume designed by Christian Lacroix, embroidered in the studios of the master embroiderer François Lesage and assembled by Firmin in Madrid. Photo taken inside the actual amphitheatre in Nîmes, after the fight (Easter 1992). Photo © Christian Courrèges.
Backstage at the Firmin studios in Madrid, the pink and yellow capes of the Spanish bullfighters. Photo © Peter Müller published in *Oro Plata, habits de lumière.*

New Year wishes. Every year Christian Lacroix produces a card specially on the theme of the Macarena, the Virgin of Seville, interpreted here by the painter David Rochline. © Christian Lacroix.
'Cascade'. Haute Couture Spring/Summer Collection 1990. Jerkin in painted Lycra and embroidered chartreuse. Photo © Mario Testino.

Choker in gilded metal, molten glass, fragments of hard stones and multicoloured rhinestones. Haute Couture Collection Spring/Summer 1995. Photo © Laziz Hamani.
Breastplate in gilded metal, Haute Couture Autumn/Winter 1991–92. Photo © Laziz Hamani.

In his studio. Christian Lacroix surrounded by some of the many ingredients that go into his collections. Photographed by Jean-Marie Perier for *Elle* magazine. Spring 1995. Photo © Jean-Marie Perier – SCOOP/*Elle*.

'Wild Oats'. Chartreuse and white 'gingham' stitched jacket, with mustard gazar basque and collar covered in embroidered black lace, worn over a straight skirt in chartreuse lamé (Haute Couture Spring/Summer 1991). Photo © Roxanne Lowit.
Sketch for the luxury Ready-to-Wear Spring/Summer Collection 1988. A yellow quilted dress with giant roses. Drawing by Christian Lacroix. © Christian Lacroix.

Carnaby Street fashions during the sixties are a source of nostalgic regret for Lacroix and remain a recurrent theme in his collections. This is his very first ready-to-wear collection (Autumn/Winter 1988–89). Knitted jacket and skirt with flounce and knitted mini dress with rosettes and pill-box hat in felt and suede. Illustration © Jean-Philippe Delhomme.

'Bain de soleil' jackets, fastened with brooches and gold crosses, made of printed lamé patchwork and large plastic discs, worn over striped T-shirts in various knits. Photo © Roxanne Lowit.

Rich and poor are combined in these pyjamas made from gold and string woven together by Madame Pouzieux, with fringe trousers. Photo © Bettina Rheims for AFM Paris, 1989.

Detail from the back: a sculpture in flax and string, photographed by Keiichi Tahara. Photo © Keiichi Tahara, published in *Entrée des Fournisseurs*.

Sketch for a box jacket in white crêpe with scooped neckline, worn with a black calf-length wraparound skirt. © Christian Lacroix.

Photomontage. The same design worn by Barbara Jackson. Montage by Gilles Élie for Lacroix's Ready-to-Wear catalogue, Spring/Summer 1996. Photo ©. Tyen.

'Bazar' Collection. Sketch by Christian Lacroix for the Autumn/Winter Ready-to-Wear Collection 1994–95. This was not thought of as a secondary line, but as a line that could be at once autonomous yet complementary and could coexist with both Ready-to-Wear and Haute Couture. © Christian Lacroix.

Time and the USA, 1988. Against all expectations, Christian Lacroix is awarded this supreme accolade following his second Haute Couture Collection in February 1988. Only Christian Dior in his time and Giorgio Armani, after years of success, achieved such a distinction. © TIME, February 1988, photo Julio Donoso.

'Syracuse': a hooded jacket in pink gazar embroidered with flowers, worn over all-in-one navy blue shantung culottes (Haute Couture Spring/Summer 1989). Photo © Roxanne Lowit.

'Parisian gaiety': Christian Lacroix designed these costumes at the time of his emergence on the American fashion scene. Using Offenbach's music, Leonid Massine choreographed the piece, which was restaged in 1988 by his son at the Metropolitan Opera in New York, and by Mikhail Baryshnikov at the American Ballet Theatre. Photo © Marta Swope, LIFE.

The finale. Christian Lacroix surrounded by his models at the end of the 1995 Haute Couture Spring/Summer show, which took place at the Grand Hotel in Paris, January 1995. Photo © Roxanne Lowit.

Acknowledgments

The publisher would like to thank the house of Christian Lacroix for their help in the realization of this work and in particular Jean-Jacques Picart, Franck Vanhille and Lars Nilsson.

Thanks also to Irving Penn, Steven Meisel, Mario Testino, Paolo Roversi, Javier Vallhonrat, Bettina Rheims, Roxanne Lowit, Dominique Issermann, Jean-Marie Perier, Marc Hispard, Keiichi Tahara, Noëlle Hoeppe, Mr Tyen, Laziz Hamani and Philippe Sebirot, Christian Courrèges, Gilles de Chabaneix, Jean-François Gaté, Jean-Philippe Delhomme, Tiziano Magni, Marta Swope, Julio Donoso, Abbas, B. Delgado, Elie/Vermersch and Peter Müller.

Also to Shalom, Christy Turlington, Trish Goff, Barbara Jackson, Véronica, Olga, Francine Howel, Marie Seznec, Claudia Mason, Marie-Sophie, Kadija, Simone D'Alliancour-Benazeraf.

Finally, this book would have been impossible without the help of Marc Vachette (Cosmos), Jean-Maurice Rouquette (Musée Réattu, Arles), Mme Gallege (Rapho), Marie-Christine Biebuyck (Magnum Photo), Lorraine Mead (*Vogue* US), Sylviane, Nanou and Colette Guérineau (Scoop), Sandrine Bleu (Parfums Christian Dior), Thierry Kauffmann, Vincent (Marion de Beaupré), Sandrine (Michèle Filoméno), Mimi Brown and Kelly O'Neil (A+C Anthology), Xavier Moreau, Valérie (Agence Philippe Arnaud), Renza (Vietri & Tartarini); also Sabine Killinger (Elite), Jean-Marc (Marilyn Agency), Marie-Louise (Pauline's), Kathryn Brandt (Turly Production).

We hope they will accept this expression of our sincere gratitude.